Marketing Analytics

Ricardo Moreno

Copyright Page

Publisher: Flamenco
Release Year 2025

Index

Marketing Analytics 7
Fundamentals 14
Data Collection and Management 21
Market Segmentation 27
KPIs and Metrics in Marketing 34
Advertising Campaign Analysis 41
Web Analytics and Digital Media 49
Analytics in Email Marketing 57
Sales and Conversion Analysis 65
Customer Lifetime Value (CLV) 73
Predictive Models and Machine Learning 81
Competitive Analysis 89
Using Analytics for Product Innovation 96
Return on Investment (ROI) Analysis 103
Privacy in Marketing Analytics 110
Future of Analytics 117

Marketing Analytics

Marketing analytics is a powerful tool that enables businesses to make informed, strategic decisions. It involves collecting, measuring, and analyzing data to understand the effectiveness of marketing activities and how they impact business goals. Through marketing analytics, we can break down complex interactions between consumers and advertising campaigns, uncovering what works and what doesn't.

Imagine you own an online store that sells clothing. Every day, hundreds of people visit your website, but not all of them make a purchase. Marketing analytics helps you understand why some people buy and others don't. By analyzing data like how long they spend on your site, what pages they visit, what products they add to their cart, and where they abandon the checkout process, you can identify patterns and behaviors. For example, you might find that many users abandon their cart when they reach the checkout page. With this information, you can make specific changes to improve that stage, such as simplifying the checkout process or offering additional payment options.

In addition to understanding user behavior on your website, marketing analytics allows you to evaluate the performance of your advertising campaigns. You can see how many people click on your ads, how long they stay on your site after clicking, and whether they take any meaningful action like signing up for your newsletter or making a purchase. This information is vital to fine-tuning your advertising strategies and optimizing your return on investment (ROI). For example, if you find that a social media campaign is bringing in a lot of traffic but few sales, you might decide to invest more in another campaign that is performing better.

Segmentation is another key area where marketing analytics plays a crucial role. Not all of your customers are the same, and it's important to recognize the differences so you can target them effectively. Using segmentation, you can group your customers into different categories based on characteristics such as demographics, purchasing behavior, interests, and preferences. You can then customize your messages and offers to each segment, thereby increasing the relevance and effectiveness of your campaigns. For example, you could create specific campaigns for returning customers that offer exclusive discounts, while sending new customers welcome promotions.

Sales and conversion analysis is critical to understanding the success of your marketing efforts. It's not just about knowing how many sales were made, but about digging into the details that lead to those sales. By examining your sales funnel, you can identify where potential customers drop out of the process and why. This allows you to make fine-tuned adjustments to improve your conversion rate. Let's say you notice a high drop-off rate at the product selection stage; you could improve product presentation, add customer reviews, or offer personalized recommendations to make the purchasing decision easier.

Customer lifetime value (CLV) is an essential metric that helps you understand how much a customer is worth to your business over time. Calculating CLV allows you to make smarter decisions about how much to spend on acquiring new customers and how to retain existing ones. If you know that an average customer spends a certain amount of money at your store over their lifetime, you can determine how much you can invest in marketing campaigns to attract and keep those customers. Plus, by identifying your most valuable customers, you can target loyalty strategies specific to them, such as loyalty programs or special discounts.

Marketing analytics also extends to competitor analysis. By studying what your competitors are doing, you can identify opportunities and threats in the market. This includes analyzing their marketing strategies, their product offerings, and how they interact with their customers. With this information, you can adjust your own strategies to stand out and gain a competitive advantage. For example, if you notice that a competitor is having success with a specific social media campaign, you could implement a similar strategy tailored to your brand and audience.

Ethics and privacy are important considerations in marketing analytics. It's crucial to handle customer data responsibly and comply with privacy regulations, such as the GDPR in Europe or the CCPA in California. This is not only a legal obligation, but also a way to build and maintain the trust of your customers. Transparency in how you collect and use data, as well as offering options for customers to control their information, are best practices.

Finally, the future of marketing analytics looks exciting with the advancement of technologies such as artificial intelligence and big data. These tools allow for deeper and more predictive analysis, helping businesses anticipate trends and consumer behaviors. For example, the use of machine learning algorithms can predict which products will be most popular in certain seasons, allowing you to better plan your inventories and marketing strategies.

Marketing analytics isn't just about looking back to understand what's worked and what hasn't, but also about using those insights to foresee the future and be better prepared. Implementing a data-driven decision-making culture can transform your business, taking you to new levels of efficiency and success. With the right tools and techniques, you can turn data into valuable insights and those insights into actions that drive your business forward.

Fundamentals

To understand marketing analytics, we must first understand its basic fundamentals. These principles are essential for anyone who wants to make the most of the tools and techniques available in this field. Marketing analytics is based on the collection, interpretation, and use of data to make informed decisions that improve our marketing strategies.

First, let's talk about data. In marketing, data is the raw material. It all starts with collecting data, which can come from a variety of sources: our own sales platforms, social media interactions, visits to our website, customer surveys, and more. Every customer touchpoint generates data that, when properly collected and analyzed, can offer deep insights into their behaviors, preferences, and needs. It's as if every action our customers take is telling us a story. But to understand that story, we need to be able to collect and organize this data effectively.

Once we have the data, the next step is to clean it and prepare it for analysis. Not all the data we collect is useful; we often find duplicate, incorrect, or irrelevant information. That's why it's crucial to clean our data, removing any information that could distort our analyses. This cleaning process ensures that the decisions we make are based on accurate and reliable information. Imagine trying to put together a puzzle with pieces that don't fit together; data cleaning is what makes sure that all the pieces of our marketing puzzle fit together perfectly.

Next, it's time to analyze the data. This is where the real magic of marketing analytics comes in. We use a variety of techniques and tools to transform that data into useful information. This can include descriptive analytics, which tells us what happened; diagnostic analytics, which helps us understand why it happened; predictive analytics, which allows us to anticipate what might happen in the future; and prescriptive analytics, which suggests specific actions to improve our results. Each of these approaches gives us unique and valuable insight into our marketing efforts.

Marketing analytics tools are varied and constantly evolving. From simple spreadsheets to advanced data analysis software, there is a wide range of options available. Tools like Google Analytics allow us to track and analyze web traffic, while CRM platforms like Salesforce help us manage and analyze our interactions with customers. Choosing the right tools depends on our specific needs and the resources available. The important thing to know is that no matter which tool we use, the end goal is the same: to turn data into valuable information that drives our marketing decisions.

Now, one of the most important concepts in marketing analytics is measuring performance through metrics and KPIs (Key Performance Indicators). Metrics help us quantify different aspects of our marketing campaigns, such as the number of visits to our website, the conversion rate of visitors to buyers, or the return on investment (ROI) of our advertising campaigns. KPIs, on the other hand, are specific metrics that we have identified as the most critical to the success of our marketing objectives. For example, if our goal is to increase sales, the most relevant KPI might be the conversion rate. Measuring and monitoring these indicators allows us to evaluate the success of our strategies and make adjustments when necessary.

Another cornerstone of marketing analytics is market segmentation. Not all customers are the same, and treating them all the same can be ineffective. Market segmentation involves dividing our customers into smaller, homogeneous groups based on shared characteristics, such as demographics, purchasing behavior, or interests. This allows us to customize our marketing campaigns to better resonate with each segment. For example, a company that sells clothing can segment its customers based on age and preferred style, and then create campaigns specific to each group. Segmentation improves the relevance and effectiveness of our marketing strategies.

Furthermore, marketing analytics not only focuses on the results of our current actions, but also on future planning. Using predictive analytics and forecasting models, we can anticipate future trends and behaviors. This allows us to stay one step ahead, adjusting our marketing strategies before significant market changes occur. For example, if a predictive analysis indicates that a particular product will be in high demand in the coming months, we can increase production and prepare specific marketing campaigns to capitalize on that anticipated demand.

Finally, it's important to note that marketing analytics is an ongoing process. It's not something we do once and then forget about; it requires constant monitoring and regular adjustments. The market changes, customer preferences evolve, and technologies advance. To stay competitive, we must always be on the lookout for these changes and adapt our strategies accordingly. Marketing analytics provides us with the tools and insights necessary to make these adjustments effectively and in a data-driven manner.

In short, the fundamentals of marketing analytics revolve around collecting and managing data, using analytical tools, measuring performance through metrics and KPIs, segmenting the market, planning for the future using predictive analytics, and maintaining a continuous and adaptive approach. These principles are essential for any company that wants to use data to improve its marketing strategies and ultimately achieve its business goals.

Data Collection and Management

Collecting and managing data is one of the most important tasks in marketing analytics. Think of data as the ingredients in a recipe. If you want to prepare a delicious meal, you need to have the best ingredients and know how to handle them. Similarly, to make sound marketing decisions, you need accurate and well-organized data. In this chapter, we'll explore how to collect and manage data effectively, and why it's crucial to the success of your marketing strategies.

First, let's talk about data collection. Data can come from a variety of sources, and each offers a different piece of the puzzle. For example, your website is a rich source of data. You can track how many people visit your site, which pages they view, how long they stay on each page, and from which devices they access it. Tools like Google Analytics are essential for this type of tracking. Then, there's social media. Platforms like Facebook, Instagram, and Twitter not only allow you to engage with your customers, but they also offer you valuable data about their behaviors and interests. Additionally, your own email marketing campaigns can provide insights into who opens your emails, who clicks on links, and who ends up buying something. All of these sources together give you a complete view of how customers interact with your brand.

However, collecting data is just the first step. What comes next is managing that data. This involves organizing and storing the data in a way that is useful and accessible. A well-designed database is essential. Imagine your database is like a library. If all the books were scattered in random piles, finding the information you need would be nearly impossible. But if the books are sorted into categories and labeled correctly, you can find what you are looking for in seconds. The same goes for data. You need a system that allows you to store the data in a structured way that is easy to query.

Part of data management also involves data cleansing. Not all of the data you collect will be useful. Sometimes, there will be duplicate, incorrect, or irrelevant data that can skew your analytics. Data cleansing is the process of identifying and removing these errors. It's like filtering water to remove impurities. You only want to work with data that is accurate and relevant to your marketing goals. For example, if you have multiple entries for the same customer due to typing errors or duplicate records, you need to consolidate that information into a single, clean, accurate entry.

Once your data is clean and organized, it's important to make sure it's protected. Data security is a critical aspect of data management. Your customer data is valuable and sensitive, and it's your responsibility to protect that information from unauthorized access or security breaches. This can include using encryption, firewalls, and other security methods to ensure that data is safe. Additionally, you must comply with privacy regulations, such as the GDPR in Europe or the CCPA in California, that dictate how you can collect, store, and use customer data.

Data management also involves keeping data up to date. Customer information can change over time, and it's crucial that your data reflects these changes. For example, if a customer changes their email address, you need to update that information in your database to ensure your communications remain effective. Similarly, if a customer's preferences change, you need to update that information to continue to offer them relevant, personalized content.

Another important aspect of data management is the integration of data from different sources. You are likely to use multiple tools and platforms to collect data, and it is essential that all this information is integrated in a cohesive manner. This will allow you to have a unified and complete view of your customers. There are various data integration tools that can help you consolidate information from different sources into a single, centralized database. This integration not only makes data analysis easier but also improves the accuracy and consistency of the information.

Finally, effective data management also involves creating reports and data visualizations. Once you have your data organized and clean, you need to be able to interpret and present it in a way that is useful for decision making. Data visualizations, such as charts and tables, can help you see patterns and trends more clearly. Tools like Tableau or Power BI are great for creating interactive visualizations that make data easier to understand. Regular reports can provide updates on the performance of your marketing campaigns and help you identify areas that need adjustments.

In conclusion, data collection and management are critical to any successful marketing strategy. It's not just about having a lot of data, but about making sure that data is accurate, relevant, and accessible. By implementing effective data collection and management practices, you can gain valuable insights that will allow you to make informed decisions and continually improve your marketing efforts. Remember that data is one of your company's most valuable assets, and managing it properly is key to unlocking its full potential.

Market Segmentation

Market segmentation is a fundamental strategy for personalizing and improving our marketing campaigns. Instead of treating all of our customers the same, segmentation allows us to divide our market into smaller, more homogeneous groups. Each group, or segment, shares similar characteristics, allowing us to tailor our strategies and messages specifically to them. This not only improves the relevance of our campaigns, but also increases the effectiveness of our marketing actions.

To start, let's think about why market segmentation is important. Imagine that you own a clothing store that sells both formal suits and sportswear. If you were to send the same ad to all of your customers, many of them would find it irrelevant. Some may be interested only in sportswear, while others may be looking for formal suits. By segmenting your market, you can send suit ads to those interested in formal wear and sportswear promotions to sports enthusiasts. Not only does this increase the likelihood that customers will respond positively, but it also makes them feel understood and valued.

There are different criteria for segmenting the market. One of the most common is demographic segmentation, which divides customers based on characteristics such as age, gender, income, educational level, and marital status. For example, a toy company might segment its market based on the age of children, offering different products for babies, toddlers, and pre-teens. Demographic segmentation is useful because these characteristics often influence consumer needs and preferences.

Another way to segment your market is through geographic segmentation, which groups customers based on their location. This can be as broad as countries and regions, or as specific as cities and neighborhoods. Geographic segmentation is particularly useful for local businesses or those that operate in multiple regions with different cultural and climatic characteristics. For example, a clothing store might promote coats and jackets in cold regions and swimwear in coastal areas during the same season.

Psychographic segmentation is another powerful technique. It is based on consumers' lifestyles, interests, values, and personalities. For example, a company that sells beauty products can segment its market based on customers who are concerned with natural and organic products versus those interested in the latest technological innovations in cosmetics. Psychographic segmentation allows for a deeper understanding of customers' purchasing motivators, making it easier to create more resonant and effective marketing messages.

Additionally, segmentation based on consumer behavior groups customers based on their actions and purchasing patterns. This includes aspects such as purchase frequency, brand loyalty, product usage, and response to previous campaigns. For example, an online store can identify customers who buy frequently and offer them loyalty programs or exclusive discounts. On the other hand, those who have only purchased once can be given incentives to make a second purchase. This type of segmentation is particularly valuable because it is based on real behavioral data, which can more accurately predict future customer actions.

Technology has made market segmentation much easier. Data analytics tools and customer relationship management (CRM) platforms allow us to collect and analyze vast amounts of information about our customers. For example, by using cookies and online behavioral tracking, we can gain detailed data about how customers interact with our website, what products they view, and which they purchase. This information can be used to create highly targeted and personalized segments. For example, if a customer frequently visits the athletic shoes section of our website but never makes a purchase, we can send them a special offer or show them personalized athletic shoe ads when they browse the Internet.

Market segmentation is not a static process; it must be continually reviewed and adjusted. As we collect more data and understand our customers better, our segments can become more precise and effective. Additionally, consumer preferences and behaviors can change over time, so it is crucial to keep up with these changes in order to adjust our marketing strategies accordingly. For example, an emerging trend in the fashion industry may lead us to create a new market segment for those interested in specific styles that we had not previously considered.

Finally, it is important to measure and evaluate the success of our segmentation strategies. This involves analyzing the performance of our campaigns in each segment and making adjustments as necessary. If we notice that a particular segment is responding very well to a specific campaign, we can increase our efforts in that area. Conversely, if another segment is not responding as we expected, we need to investigate why and adjust our strategy. This ongoing evaluation allows us to optimize our marketing campaigns and maximize our return on investment.

In short, market segmentation is an essential strategy for any business that wants to improve the relevance and effectiveness of its marketing campaigns. By dividing our customers into smaller, more homogeneous groups, we can personalize our messages and offers to better resonate with each segment. Using criteria such as demographics, geography, psychographics, and behavior, we can gain a deeper understanding of our customers and create more precise and effective marketing strategies. Technology and data analytics have made this process easier, allowing us to collect and analyze detailed information about our customers. By staying flexible and adjusting to changes in consumer preferences, we can ensure that our segmentation strategies remain relevant and successful.

KPIs and Metrics in Marketing

Understanding KPIs and metrics in marketing is like having a map and compass to navigate the vast ocean of marketing campaigns. KPIs, or key performance indicators, and metrics are essential tools that help us measure the success of our strategies and make informed decisions. Without these indicators, we would be sailing blindly, not knowing if we are on the right path or if we need to adjust our course.

Let's start with the basics. Metrics are quantifiable data that show us various aspects of our marketing campaigns. They can include a wide range of information, such as the number of visits to our website, the number of clicks on an ad, email open rates, and more. KPIs, on the other hand, are specific metrics that we have identified as the most important to achieving our business objectives. Not all metrics are KPIs; only those that are directly aligned with our strategic goals are. For example, if our main goal is to increase sales, a relevant KPI could be the conversion rate – the percentage of visitors who make a purchase.

Selecting the right KPIs for your campaigns is critical. Choosing the right KPIs means understanding which aspects of performance are critical to the success of your strategy. For example, if you're running a social media campaign, you might consider KPIs like engagement (interactions), reach (number of people viewing your content), and follower growth. Each of these KPIs gives you a different perspective on the impact of your campaign and helps you identify what's working and what's not.

One of the most common KPIs in digital marketing is the conversion rate. This metric tells us what percentage of visitors to our website take a specific action, such as making a purchase, signing up for a newsletter, or filling out a contact form. The conversion rate is crucial because it shows us how effective our website and our campaigns are in converting visitors into customers. For example, if we notice that our conversion rate is low, we can research and optimize elements of our page, such as the design, content, or checkout process, to improve this metric.

Another important KPI is return on investment, or ROI. ROI tells us how much we earn compared to what we spend on our marketing campaigns. To calculate it, we subtract the cost of investment from the revenue generated and then divide that amount by the cost of investment. ROI is essential because it allows us to see if our campaigns are profitable and justify the investment. For example, if we spend a thousand dollars on an advertising campaign and generate two thousand dollars in sales, our ROI would be one hundred percent, indicating that the campaign was successful.

Click-through rates, or CTR, are another important metric, especially in online advertising campaigns. CTR measures the percentage of people who click on an ad after seeing it. This metric is useful for evaluating the effectiveness of our ads and the relevance of the message to our audience. If the CTR is low, it could be a sign that we need to improve the ad design, message, or audience segmentation. On the other hand, a high CTR indicates that our ad is capturing users' attention and interest.

Social media engagement is another key KPI that measures how users interact with our content. This can include likes, comments, shares, and mentions. Engagement is crucial because it not only indicates that people are viewing our content, but that they are actively engaging with it. A high level of engagement suggests that our content resonates with our audience and fosters a stronger connection with our brand. For example, an Instagram post with a lot of likes and comments indicates that the audience finds the content interesting and valuable.

Bounce rate is a metric that measures the percentage of visitors who leave our website after viewing just one page. A high bounce rate can be worrying as it suggests that visitors aren't finding what they're looking for or aren't interested in the content. This can be due to a number of factors, such as poor user experience, irrelevant content, or slow loading times. By monitoring and reducing bounce rate, we can improve visitor retention and increase the chances of converting visitors into customers.

Cost per acquisition, or CPA, is another key KPI that measures how much it costs us to acquire a new customer through our marketing campaigns. To calculate CPA, we divide the total cost of the campaign by the number of new customer acquisitions. This metric is essential for assessing the efficiency of our campaigns and ensuring that we are spending our resources effectively. For example, if we find that our CPA is too high, we can look for ways to optimize our campaigns to reduce costs and improve efficiency.

In addition to these specific KPIs, it's important to consider cohort analysis, which allows us to group users based on a shared characteristic and analyze their behavior over time. This can provide us with deeper insights into how different groups of customers interact with our brand and respond to our campaigns. For example, we might analyze the behavior of users who signed up during a specific promotion and compare it to those who signed up at other times. This type of analysis helps us identify patterns and trends that can influence our future strategies.

Finally, it's crucial to remember that KPIs and metrics are not static. We must regularly review and adjust them to reflect changes in our goals and the market environment. Continuously monitoring and evaluating our KPIs allows us to quickly identify any issues and make the necessary adjustments to keep our campaigns on track. For example, if we notice a drop in social media engagement, we can investigate the causes and test new tactics to regain our audience's interest.

In conclusion, KPIs and metrics are essential tools in marketing that help us measure the success of our campaigns and make informed decisions. By selecting the right KPIs and regularly monitoring our metrics, we can optimize our marketing strategies and achieve our goals more effectively. These indicators provide us with clear guidance on what is working and what is not, allowing us to adjust our approach and continually improve. Understanding and using KPIs and metrics effectively is key to the success of any marketing campaign.

Advertising Campaign Analysis

Advertising campaign analysis is a powerful tool for any business that wants to ensure that their advertising investment is paying off. Analyzing our campaigns not only helps us understand how effective they are, but also helps us identify areas for improvement and optimize our future strategies. In this chapter, we'll explore step-by-step how to conduct a thorough analysis of advertising campaigns, using a simple and straightforward approach to ensure that we're getting the most benefit from our advertising efforts.

To start, it's essential to be clear about the goals of our campaign before launching it. Do we want to increase sales? Are we looking to drive more traffic to our website? Do we want to improve brand awareness? Each goal will have its own success indicators and specific metrics that we need to track. For example, if our goal is to increase sales, key metrics will include conversion rate and return on investment. If we're looking to drive more traffic, we should focus on the number of website visits and click-through rate on our ads. Having clear goals will allow us to focus our analysis on the most relevant data.

Once we have set our goals, the next step is to collect the data. We will use various analytics tools such as Google Analytics for web traffic, social media platforms for engagement and impressions, and advertising-specific tools such as Google Ads or Facebook Ads to get detailed data on the performance of our ads. This data collection phase is crucial as it provides us with the basis on which we will conduct all our analysis. It is important to ensure that the data is accurate and up to date.

With the data in hand, we begin the analysis process. A good place to start is by reviewing basic metrics such as impressions, clicks, and conversions. Impressions tell us how many times our ad was shown, while clicks show us how many people clicked on it. Conversions, on the other hand, tell us how many of those people took the desired action, such as making a purchase or signing up for a newsletter. These basic metrics give us an overview of how our campaign is performing.

However, to gain a deeper understanding, we need to go beyond basic metrics. This is where conversion rate analysis becomes important. The conversion rate shows us the percentage of people who took the desired action after clicking on our ad. If this rate is low, it may be a sign that something on our landing page isn't working well. Maybe the page takes too long to load, or perhaps the content isn't persuasive enough. By identifying these issues, we can make the necessary adjustments to improve the effectiveness of our campaigns.

Another key metric to look at is cost per click, or CPC. This metric shows us how much we are paying, on average, for each click on our ad. A high CPC can indicate that we are competing in a very saturated market, which may require a review of our bidding strategy or the exploration of less competitive keywords. Additionally, we need to consider cost per acquisition, or CPA, which tells us how much we are spending on average to acquire a new customer. If the CPA is too high compared to the customer lifetime value, we may need to adjust our strategy to improve profitability.

Audience segmentation analysis is also crucial. We need to examine how different segments of our audience are responding to our ads. For example, are our ads having more success among certain demographic groups? Are there specific regions where ads are driving more conversions? By understanding these variations, we can adjust our campaigns to focus more on the segments that are responding best and reconfigure our messaging for those that aren't having the same impact.

Additionally, it is important to analyze the performance of our ads on different channels. If we are using multiple platforms, such as Google Ads, Facebook Ads, and display advertising, we should compare the performance on each of them. Some platforms may be more effective than others depending on our audience and the types of products or services we are promoting. This analysis allows us to reallocate our budget more efficiently, investing more in the channels that are generating better results.

Campaign length can also impact campaign performance. It's useful to analyze how ad performance varies over time. For example, there may be a spike in activity during certain days of the week or times of day. By identifying these patterns, we can schedule our ads to run at the most effective times, thereby maximizing our ad spend. Additionally, if we notice ad performance declining over time, it may be a sign that audiences are developing ad fatigue and need to be refreshed with new creative or messaging.

Another important aspect of campaign analysis is tracking ROI. We need to compare the total cost of the campaign to the revenue generated to determine if we are getting a positive return. This analysis not only helps us understand the profitability of the campaign, but also provides us with valuable insights for planning future investments. If a specific campaign has a high ROI, we can consider replicating that strategy in the future. Conversely, if a campaign is not generating the expected return, we need to investigate the reasons and adjust our tactics accordingly.

Finally, we need to consider qualitative analysis as well as quantitative analysis. This involves reviewing customer comments and feedback on our ads. Customer reviews can provide valuable insights into how our ads are perceived and what aspects could be improved. For example, if multiple customers mention that an ad is confusing or unattractive, it's a sign that we need to work on our messaging or design. Qualitative analysis helps us understand the emotional impact of our ads and create campaigns that resonate better with our audience.

In short, advertising campaign analysis is a comprehensive process that helps us understand and improve the effectiveness of our marketing strategies. By setting clear goals, collecting and analyzing detailed data, and making adjustments based on the results, we can maximize the impact of our campaigns and ensure we are getting the best possible return on our advertising investment. This approach allows us to not only improve our current campaigns, but also learn and grow, continually adapting to the changing needs and preferences of our audience.

Web Analytics and Digital Media

Web and digital media analytics have become an indispensable tool for any business looking to thrive in today's digital environment. This process involves collecting, measuring, and analyzing data from our online activities to better understand how users interact with our digital content and how we can optimize our strategies to achieve better results. In this chapter, we will explore in detail how web and digital media analytics can transform our marketing campaigns and help us make more informed decisions.

Let's start with the basics: what is web analytics? In simple terms, it's the process of tracking and analyzing what visitors do on our website. We use tools like Google Analytics to collect data on site traffic, most visited pages, time spent on each page, conversion rates, and other key metrics. This information allows us to understand user behavior and improve the website experience.

To get started, it's essential to install an analytics tool on our website. Google Analytics is a popular, free option that offers a wide range of functionality. Once we've set up Google Analytics, we can begin tracking a variety of metrics. For example, we can see how many people visit our website daily, where those visits come from, and what devices they use to access the site. This basic information gives us an overview of our website traffic and helps us identify trends.

One of the most important metrics we need to monitor is the number of visits. This metric tells us how many people are visiting our website in a specific time period. However, it's not enough to know how many people are visiting our site; it's also crucial to understand how they got there. This is where traffic source analysis comes into play. We can see whether visits are coming from organic search, paid ads, social media, emails, or direct links. This information helps us evaluate the effectiveness of our different marketing strategies and adjust our efforts accordingly.

Another key metric is the bounce rate. This rate shows us the percentage of visitors who leave our website after viewing just one page. A high bounce rate can be a sign that something isn't working well on our site. Maybe the homepage isn't attractive enough, or users aren't finding what they're looking for easily. Analyzing the bounce rate allows us to identify problems and make improvements to keep visitors on the site longer.

Time on site and pages per session are other important metrics. These tell us how much time users spend on our website and how many pages they visit during a single session. Higher time on site and more pages per session generally indicate that users find our content valuable and are interested in exploring more. If these metrics are low, it could be a sign that we need to improve the content or navigation of the site to keep users staying longer and exploring more pages.

Conversion rates are essential to measuring the success of our campaigns. A conversion can be any action we want users to take, such as making a purchase, signing up for a newsletter, or filling out a contact form. By tracking conversion rates, we can see what percentage of visitors are completing these actions and how we can improve our site to increase conversions. For example, if we notice that many people are abandoning their shopping cart before completing a purchase, we might investigate and improve the checkout process to make it easier and faster.

Digital media analytics is not limited to our website; it also includes our activities on social media and other digital platforms. Social media is an integral part of our digital marketing strategies, and it is crucial to track and analyze our performance on these platforms. Tools like Facebook Insights, Twitter Analytics, and LinkedIn Analytics provide us with valuable data on how users interact with our content on these networks. We can view metrics such as reach, impressions, engagements, and follower growth.

Reach shows us how many people have seen our content, while impressions indicate how many times the content has been shown. Interactions, which include likes, comments, shares, and clicks, show us how users are engaging with our content.

Analyzing these metrics helps us understand what type of content resonates most with our audience and how we can adjust our posts to improve engagement.

Digital advertising campaign analysis is another crucial area. We use platforms like Google Ads and Facebook Ads to create and manage advertising campaigns, and these platforms provide us with a wealth of data to analyze. We can view metrics like cost per click, cost per acquisition, click-through rate, and conversions. By analyzing these metrics, we can evaluate the effectiveness of our campaigns and make adjustments to improve performance.

For example, if we notice that an ad has a high cost per click but few conversions, it could be a sign that the ad is not well-targeted or that the landing page is not effective. In this case, we could test different creatives, adjust the audience targeting, or improve the landing page to see if we can get better results. The ability to perform A/B testing is a significant advantage in digital advertising, as it allows us to compare different versions of ads and see which one performs best.

In addition to analyzing our individual campaigns, it's important to look at the bigger picture. This includes analyzing trends over time and comparing performance across different channels. For example, we can compare organic search traffic to paid ad traffic to see which is more effective at attracting visitors. We can also analyze how user behavior varies across different devices, such as desktop, tablet, and mobile. This information helps us adjust our strategies to maximize impact across each channel and device.

Qualitative data analysis is also essential. This involves reviewing user comments and feedback on our website and social media. User opinions and suggestions provide us with valuable insight into what they like and dislike about our content and brand. For example, if several users mention that they find our website difficult to navigate, we can take steps to improve the structure and usability. Qualitative analysis helps us humanize the data and better understand the needs and expectations of our audience.

In short, web and digital media analytics is a powerful tool that allows us to better understand our audience, optimize our strategies, and make more informed decisions. By tracking and analyzing a variety of metrics, we can identify what's working and what's not, and make adjustments as necessary to improve our performance. This data-driven approach allows us to be more efficient and effective in our marketing strategies, ensuring that we are maximizing the return on our investment and delivering the best possible experience to our users. Web and digital media analytics is a constantly evolving discipline, and keeping up with the latest tools and techniques will help us stay competitive in the ever-changing digital landscape.

Analytics in Email Marketing

Email marketing analytics is one of the most valuable tools we have at our disposal to understand and optimize our email campaigns. Despite the growing popularity of social media and other forms of digital communication, email remains an effective way to reach our customers. However, to get the most out of this tool, it is essential to carefully analyze the performance of our email marketing campaigns. In this chapter, we will explore how to perform this analysis in a simple and specific way, providing clear strategies to improve our results.

The first step in email marketing analytics is to understand the basic metrics we need to track. Core metrics include open rate, click rate, bounce rate, and conversion rate. Each of these metrics provides us with valuable insights into different aspects of our email campaigns and helps us identify areas for improvement.

The open rate is perhaps the most basic but also one of the most important metrics. It tells us how many people opened our email compared to the total number of emails sent. A low open rate can be a sign that our subject lines are not engaging enough or that our emails are ending up in recipients' spam folders. To improve the open rate, it is crucial to work on writing eye-catching and relevant subject lines, and to make sure that we are sending emails to contact lists that really want to receive our information.

Click-through rate shows us how many people clicked on one or more links within our email. This metric is essential to understand the level of engagement our recipients have with the content of the email. While a high open rate is a good indicator, what really matters is whether recipients are interacting with the content. To improve click-through rate, we need to make sure our emails are visually appealing and contain clear and compelling calls to action. Additionally, it is useful to segment our contact list to send more personalized and relevant content.

The bounce rate tells us the percentage of emails that could not be delivered to the recipients. There are two types of bounces: hard bounces and soft bounces. Hard bounces occur when the email cannot be delivered due to invalid or non-existent addresses, while soft bounces occur for temporary reasons, such as full mailboxes or server problems. A high bounce rate can negatively affect our sending reputation, so it is crucial to keep our contact list clean and up to date. By regularly removing invalid addresses and managing soft bounces, we can improve our delivery rate and ensure that our emails reach their intended recipients.

Conversion rate is perhaps the metric most directly related to the ROI of our email marketing campaigns. It tells us how many people took the desired action after clicking a link in our email, whether it was making a purchase, registering for an event, or filling out a form. To improve conversion rate, we need to make sure our landing pages are optimized and consistent with the content of the email. Additionally, using A/B testing for different elements of the email, such as the design, content, and call to action, can help us identify what works best for our audience.

Once we've understood and started tracking these basic metrics, it's important to dig deeper into the analysis to get a more complete understanding of the performance of our email marketing campaigns. For example, we can analyze recipient behavior based on different segments of our contact list. How do open and click rates vary across different demographic groups? Are there significant differences in engagement between new subscribers and long-term subscribers? This type of analysis allows us to customize our campaigns for different segments and improve the relevance of the content we send.

Send timing analysis can also provide valuable insights. By reviewing data from our past campaigns, we can identify patterns in which days and times our emails perform best. For example, we might find that emails sent on Tuesday mornings have a significantly higher open rate than those sent on Friday afternoons. By adjusting our send times based on these patterns, we can maximize the likelihood that our emails will be opened and read.

Another powerful tool in email marketing analytics is user path tracking. By tracking recipients' behavior after they click a link in our email, we can gain a deeper understanding of their experience and any obstacles they may be facing. For example, if we notice that many users click a link but leave the landing page without completing a conversion, it could be a sign that the landing page needs improvement. Maybe the page is too complicated, or the conversion process isn't clear enough. By addressing these issues, we can significantly improve our conversion rates.

Content analysis is another crucial aspect. By reviewing which types of content drive the most clicks and conversions, we can adjust our content strategies to focus on what really resonates with our audience. For example, if we notice that emails that include how-to guides or case studies perform better than promotional emails, we can adjust our approach to include more of that type of content. Additionally, using visual elements, such as images and videos, can increase engagement and make our emails more engaging.

Finally, it is essential to measure the ROI of our email marketing campaigns. This involves comparing the cost of creating and sending our emails with the revenue generated by the resulting conversions. By having a clear view of our ROI, we can justify our email marketing budget and make adjustments to maximize profitability. If a specific campaign has a high ROI, we can consider replicating that strategy in future campaigns. On the other hand, if a campaign is not generating the expected return, we need to investigate the reasons and adjust our tactics accordingly.

In short, email marketing analytics is a powerful tool that allows us to better understand the performance of our campaigns and make adjustments to improve results. By tracking and analyzing a variety of metrics, we can identify what is working and what is not, and make informed decisions to optimize our strategies. This data-driven approach allows us to be more efficient and effective in our email marketing campaigns, ensuring that we are maximizing the return on our investment and offering the best possible experience to our subscribers. Email marketing analytics is a constantly evolving discipline, and keeping up with the latest tools and techniques will help us stay competitive in the ever-changing digital landscape.

Sales and Conversion Analysis

Sales and conversion analysis is a fundamental tool for any company that wants to better understand its performance and optimize its marketing and sales strategies. In this chapter, we will explore in detail how to perform this analysis effectively, using simple terms and clear strategies to help you improve your results.

To start, it's essential to understand what conversion means in the context of sales. A conversion can be any action we want a potential customer to take, such as purchasing a product, signing up for a service, filling out a contact form, or downloading a resource. Conversion analysis helps us measure how many people are taking these actions compared to the total number of visitors or prospects.

One of the first metrics we need to consider is the conversion rate, which is the percentage of visitors who complete the desired action. To calculate the conversion rate, we simply divide the number of conversions by the total number of visitors and then multiply by 100 to get a percentage. For example, if 1,000 people visit our website and 50 of them make a purchase, our conversion rate would be 5 percent. This metric gives us an overview of the effectiveness of our marketing and sales strategies.

However, conversion rate alone doesn't give us all the information we need. It's important to break down the data to gain a more detailed understanding. For example, we can analyze the conversion rate across different segments of our market. How does the conversion rate vary between different demographic groups, such as age, gender, or geographic location? What differences are there between new visitors and returning visitors? This type of analysis helps us identify patterns and opportunities to customize our strategies and improve conversion in specific segments.

Another crucial metric is the average order value, which tells us how much customers spend on average per transaction. This value is calculated by dividing total revenue by the number of orders. If our average order value is low, we might consider strategies to increase each customer's spending, such as offering complementary products, volume discounts, or loyalty programs. By increasing the average order value, we can increase our revenue without needing to attract more visitors.

Conversion funnel analysis is another powerful tool. A conversion funnel is a model that describes the process potential customers follow from first contact with our brand to final conversion. This funnel can have several stages, such as awareness, interest, consideration, and decision. By analyzing each stage of the funnel, we can identify where we are losing potential customers and take steps to improve those areas.

For example, if we notice that many people are abandoning their shopping cart before completing the purchase, we might investigate the reasons behind this. Maybe the checkout process is too complicated or the shipping cost is too high. By simplifying the checkout process and offering more attractive shipping options, we can reduce cart abandonment and increase our conversions. Additionally, we can use techniques like remarketing to re-engage those potential customers who abandoned their cart.

Traffic source analysis is also critical. We need to know where our visitors are coming from and which of those sources are driving the highest conversions. Traffic sources can include organic search, paid ads, social media, emails, and direct traffic. By identifying the most effective traffic sources, we can focus our efforts and resources on those areas to maximize our conversions.

For example, if we find that organic search traffic has a significantly higher conversion rate than social media traffic, we might invest more in SEO strategies to improve our search engine rankings. Similarly, if email marketing campaigns are generating a lot of conversions, we can expand our efforts in this area, sending more personalized and relevant emails to our audience.

In addition to analyzing traditional metrics, it's important to consider user behavior. Tools like heatmaps and session recordings allow us to see how users interact with our website. We can identify areas where users spend the most time, which elements draw their attention the most, and where they tend to click. This type of analysis helps us optimize the design and usability of our website to improve user experience and increase conversions.

Analyzing customer retention and repeat rates is also essential. Retention refers to a company's ability to keep its customers over time, while repeat measures how frequently customers make additional purchases. A high retention and repeat rate is a good indicator of customer satisfaction and brand loyalty. To improve these rates, we can implement loyalty programs, offer exclusive discounts to repeat customers, and maintain constant, personalized communication with our customers.

Additionally, it is helpful to conduct surveys and get direct feedback from customers. Surveys can provide us with valuable insights into the reasons why customers do or do not purchase our products. Asking customers about their shopping experience, their preferences, and any problems they have encountered helps us identify areas for improvement and adjust our strategies accordingly. This direct feedback is a powerful tool for improving customer satisfaction and increasing conversions.

Predictive analytics is another exciting and advanced area in sales and conversion analysis. Using statistical models and machine learning algorithms, we can predict future customer behavior based on historical data. For example, we can predict which customers are most likely to make a purchase in the future or which products will be most popular in the upcoming season. These predictions allow us to make more informed and proactive decisions, adjusting our marketing and sales strategies to maximize results.

It's important to remember that sales and conversion analytics isn't a one-time process; it's an ongoing cycle of measurement, analysis, and optimization. We should always be monitoring our metrics, testing, and adjusting our strategies based on the data. This iterative approach allows us to constantly improve and adapt to changes in customer and market behavior.

In conclusion, sales and conversion analytics is an essential tool for any business looking to optimize their marketing and sales strategies. By tracking and analyzing a variety of metrics, we can gain a deeper understanding of our performance, identify areas for improvement, and make more informed decisions. This data-driven approach allows us to be more efficient and effective in our strategies, ensuring that we are maximizing the return on our investment and delivering the best possible experience to our customers. Sales and conversion analytics is a constantly evolving discipline, and staying up to date with the latest tools and techniques will help us stay competitive in the ever-changing business landscape.

Customer Lifetime Value (CLV)

Customer Lifetime Value is a metric that allows us to calculate how much a customer is worth to our company over time. This metric is crucial because it helps us understand not only the immediate value of a sale, but also the long-term value that a customer can bring. Knowing Customer Lifetime Value allows us to make more informed decisions about how much we can spend on acquiring new customers and retaining existing ones.

To start, we need to understand what exactly Customer Lifetime Value is. In simple terms, it is an estimate of the total revenue a customer will generate for our company during the time they remain active with us. This includes all the purchases the customer will make from the moment they make their first purchase to their last. By knowing this figure, we can better evaluate the return on investment of our marketing strategies and make better decisions about where and how to spend our resources.

Calculating Customer Lifetime Value involves several steps. First, we need to determine the average value of a purchase.

This is calculated by dividing the total revenue generated by the number of transactions. For example, if our total revenue is $10,000 and we have had 200 transactions, the average value of a purchase would be $50. This value gives us a basic idea of how much our customers spend on each purchase.

The next step is to calculate the average purchase frequency, which is the number of purchases a customer makes in a given time period. To do this, we divide the total number of purchases by the number of unique customers. If we have 200 transactions made by 50 unique customers, the average purchase frequency would be 4. This means that, on average, each customer makes 4 purchases in the analyzed time period.

Once we have these two values, we can calculate the average value of a customer in a year. We multiply the average value of a purchase by the average purchase frequency. Continuing with our example, if the average value of a purchase is $50 and the average purchase frequency is 4, the average value of a customer in a year would be $200. This value shows us how much a customer is worth to our company in a year.

The next step is to determine the average customer lifetime, which is the length of time a customer remains active with our company. This can be estimated by analyzing our customers' purchase history. For example, if we find out that on average our customers remain active for 3 years, we can use this figure in our calculation.

Finally, to calculate Customer Lifetime Value, we multiply the average value of a customer in one year by the average customer lifetime. In our example, if the average value of a customer in one year is $200 and the average customer lifetime is 3 years, the Customer Lifetime Value would be $600. This means that, on average, each customer will generate $600 in revenue during their relationship with our company.

Knowing Customer Lifetime Value allows us to make more informed decisions about our customer acquisition and retention strategies. For example, if we know that the lifetime value of a customer is $600, we can justify spending more on acquiring new customers. If we are spending $100 on marketing to acquire a new customer and the customer lifetime value is $600, we are getting a good return on investment. This gives us the confidence to invest more in our customer acquisition campaigns, knowing that we will recoup that investment over time.

Additionally, Customer Lifetime Value helps us focus on customer retention. Keeping existing customers is generally more cost-effective than acquiring new ones. By knowing the customer lifetime value, we can implement retention strategies that help us maximize this value. This can include loyalty programs, discounts for returning customers, and excellent customer service. These strategies not only increase customer satisfaction, but also extend the customer's lifetime, thus increasing Customer Lifetime Value.

It's important to note that Customer Lifetime Value is not a static figure; it can change over time as we improve our marketing and customer service strategies. Therefore, it's crucial to review and recalculate Customer Lifetime Value regularly to ensure we're making decisions based on up-to-date data. This allows us to adjust our strategies based on changing customer trends and behaviors.

Another aspect to consider is Customer Lifetime Value segmentation. Not all customers have the same value to our company. By segmenting our customers into different groups based on their lifetime value, we can customize our marketing and retention strategies for each segment. For example, we can identify our most valuable customers and create targeted marketing campaigns to maintain their loyalty and increase their spending. Similarly, we can identify customers with lower lifetime value and work on strategies to increase their engagement and value.

Technology plays a crucial role in measuring and analyzing Customer Lifetime Value. Analytics and CRM (Customer Relationship Management) tools allow us to track customer behavior, analyze data, and calculate Customer Lifetime Value more accurately. These tools also allow us to automate our marketing campaigns and personalize them based on customer data, helping us maximize Customer Lifetime Value.

Finally, it is essential to remember that Customer Lifetime Value is a metric that reflects the overall health of our relationship with customers. A high Customer Lifetime Value number indicates that we are doing a good job in customer acquisition, retention, and satisfaction. On the other hand, a low number can be a sign that we need to review and improve our strategies. By focusing on increasing Customer Lifetime Value, we are working not only to increase our revenue, but also to build strong, long-lasting relationships with our customers.

In conclusion, Customer Lifetime Value is a fundamental metric that helps us understand the long-term value of our customers. By calculating and analyzing this metric, we can make more informed decisions about our marketing and sales strategies, focusing on customer acquisition and retention more effectively. With a data-driven approach, we can maximize the value of each customer, increase our revenue, and build long-lasting, satisfying relationships with our audience.

Predictive Models and Machine Learning

Imagine if you could predict the future of your business with a high degree of accuracy. Predictive models and machine learning allow you to do just that. These tools analyze large amounts of data to identify patterns and trends, helping you make more informed and strategic decisions. In this chapter, we'll explore how predictive models and machine learning work, and how you can use them in your marketing strategy to improve results and increase efficiency.

To start, it's essential to understand what predictive models are. A predictive model is a tool that uses historical data to predict future outcomes. For example, if you have sales data for the past five years, a predictive model can analyze that data and predict what your sales will be in the coming months. This is made possible by complex algorithms that look for patterns in the data and make predictions based on those patterns.

Machine learning is a branch of artificial intelligence that focuses on developing algorithms that enable computers to learn and make predictions or decisions based on data. Rather than being explicitly programmed to perform a task, machines use data to learn how to perform that task on their own. This means that the more data you feed a machine learning algorithm, the more accurate its predictions will be.

There are several types of machine learning algorithms, but the most common in marketing are supervised and unsupervised algorithms. Supervised algorithms use a labeled data set to learn. For example, if you want to predict which customers are most likely to buy a product, you can use a data set that includes information about customers who have and have not bought in the past. The algorithm will learn to identify the characteristics of customers who buy and apply that knowledge to predict future buyers.

On the other hand, unsupervised algorithms do not use labeled data. Instead, they look for patterns and relationships in the data without any prior knowledge. These algorithms are useful for segmenting customers into groups with similar characteristics or identifying unusual behaviors in the data. A common example is cluster analysis, which groups customers into segments based on their behaviors and characteristics.

The first step to using predictive models and machine learning in your business is to collect and prepare data. Data can come from a variety of sources, including your website, marketing campaigns, sales, social media, and more. It's important that the data is high quality, meaning it should be accurate, complete, and relevant. Once you have the data, you need to clean and format it to make sure it's suitable for analysis.

After preparing your data, the next step is to select the right predictive model. There are many different models to choose from, and choosing the right model will depend on your specific goal. For example, if you want to predict future sales, you might use a linear regression model. If you want to segment your customers, you might use a cluster model. It is often helpful to test several different models and compare their results to find the one that works best for your specific case.

Once you have selected and trained your model, you can use it to make predictions. It is important to validate the model to ensure that it is accurate and reliable. This involves testing the model on a separate data set that was not used during training to see how it performs. If the model is accurate, you can deploy it and start using it to make informed decisions.

Predictive models and machine learning have many applications in marketing. One of the most common applications is customer segmentation. By analyzing customer data, you can identify segments with similar characteristics and behaviors. This allows you to customize your marketing strategies for each segment, which can increase the effectiveness of your campaigns and improve the customer experience.

Another application is predicting customer turnover. Churn refers to the loss of customers. By analyzing historical data of customers who have stopped using your products or services, you can identify patterns and early signs of churn. This allows you to take proactive steps to retain those customers, such as offering special incentives or improving customer service.

Machine learning can also help you optimize your marketing campaigns. For example, you can use predictive models to identify which marketing messages are most effective for different customer segments. This allows you to personalize your campaigns and increase their effectiveness. Additionally, you can use machine learning to optimize budget allocation across different marketing channels, ensuring that you are spending your resources as efficiently as possible.

Personalization is another area where predictive models and machine learning can make a big difference. By analyzing customer behavioral data, you can personalize product recommendations, offers, and messages based on each customer's individual interests and needs. Not only does this improve the customer experience, but it can also increase conversion rates and customer lifetime value.

Predictive analytics can also improve inventory and supply chain management. By predicting future demand for products, you can optimize your inventory levels to avoid both overstocking and understocking. Not only does this reduce costs, but it also improves customer satisfaction by ensuring products are available when they need them.

As you implement predictive models and machine learning in your business, it's important to continually monitor and adjust your models. Customer behavior and market conditions change over time, so your models need to be regularly updated with new data to maintain their accuracy and relevance. Additionally, you should be open to trying new models and techniques as technology and methods advance.

In conclusion, predictive models and machine learning are powerful tools that can transform your marketing strategy and significantly improve your results. By using these technologies, you can gain a deeper understanding of your customers, optimize your marketing campaigns, improve customer retention, and make more informed and strategic decisions. Although it may seem challenging at first, the long-term benefits of implementing predictive models and machine learning in your business are immense and will allow you to maintain a competitive advantage in the market.

Competitive Analysis

Understanding your competition is essential to any successful marketing strategy. Competitor analysis not only helps you understand who your rivals are in the market, but also helps you identify their strengths and weaknesses, as well as the opportunities and threats they pose to your business. This knowledge allows you to adjust your strategy and find ways to differentiate yourself, offering unique value to your customers.

The first step in competitive analysis is to identify who your competitors are. These can be direct or indirect. Direct competitors are those who offer products or services similar to yours and compete for the same group of customers. Indirect competitors, on the other hand, offer products or services that can be substitutes for yours. For example, if you sell bicycles, your direct competitors are other bike shops, while indirect competitors could be scooter manufacturers or bike rental companies.

Once you have identified your competitors, the next step is to gather information about them. This information can come from a variety of sources, such as their websites, social media, financial reports, industry news, and customer reviews. You can also use market and competitor analysis tools that can provide you with valuable data on your rivals' performance.

It's important to analyze several key aspects of your competitors. First, examine their products or services. What features and benefits do they offer? How do they compare to yours in terms of quality, price, and value? Understanding these differences will help you identify opportunities to improve your own products and find ways to stand out in the marketplace.

The next thing to consider is your competitors' marketing strategy. Look at how they promote their products or services. What marketing channels do they use? What messages and tactics do they employ? Analyzing their marketing campaigns will give you insights into what works well in your industry and help you avoid mistakes that others have made. It will also allow you to identify gaps in the market that you can exploit with your own campaigns.

It's also crucial to analyze your competitors' online presence. This includes their websites, blogs, social media, and any other digital platforms they use. Evaluate the quality and content of their websites, as well as the frequency and type of posts they make on social media. Pay attention to the level of interaction and engagement they achieve with their audience. This information will help you improve your own digital marketing strategy and create more engaging and relevant content for your target audience.

Another important aspect of competitor analysis is studying your rivals' reputation and brand perception. You can do this by reviewing online customer reviews and feedback, as well as reviews on websites and social media. Pay attention to what customers value and what they criticize about your competitors. This information will give you a clear idea of their strengths and weaknesses from a customer perspective, allowing you to adjust your own strategies to better meet the needs and expectations of your audience.

In addition to analyzing your current competitors, it's important to stay abreast of trends and developments in your industry. This includes new technologies, changes in consumer preferences, and the entry of new competitors into the market. Stay informed about these trends so you can anticipate changes and adjust your strategy accordingly. You can do this by subscribing to industry newsletters, attending conferences and events, and participating in online forums and discussion groups.

Price analysis is another crucial component of competitive analysis. Compare the prices of your products or services to those of your competitors. Are you charging more, less, or about the same? Understanding how your prices are positioned in the market will help you adjust your pricing strategy to attract more customers and increase your profit margins. If you choose to compete on price, make sure your cost structure allows for it. If you prefer to compete on quality or added value, focus your marketing efforts on clearly communicating these benefits to your customers.

It is essential to not only collect data about your competitors but also to analyse them effectively. Use analysis matrices such as SWOT analysis (strengths, weaknesses, opportunities and threats) to organise the information and gain a clear view of your position in the market. Identify areas where you can improve and opportunities you can take advantage of to outperform your competitors.

Finally, remember that competitor analysis is not a one-time task; it should be an ongoing process. The market and your competitors are constantly evolving, so it is essential to regularly review and update your competitor analysis. This will allow you to always stay one step ahead and adapt your marketing strategy as market conditions change.

In conclusion, competitor analysis is a powerful tool that provides you with a deep understanding of the competitive landscape in which you operate. By identifying and analyzing your competitors, you can uncover opportunities to improve your products, adjust your marketing strategies, and offer unique value to your customers. Although it requires time and effort, competitor analysis provides you with valuable insights that will help you make more informed decisions and maintain a competitive advantage in the marketplace.

Using Analytics for Product Innovation

Analytics can be a powerful tool for product innovation. Instead of relying on intuition or guesswork alone, you can use data to guide the process of developing new products or improving existing ones. This approach not only reduces the risk associated with innovation, but also increases the likelihood of success by creating products that truly meet the needs and wants of your customers.

To get started, it's crucial to gather relevant data. This includes information about customer preferences and behaviors, market trends, and current product performance. This data can be obtained from a variety of sources, such as customer surveys, social media analysis, market research, and historical sales. Once you have this information, you can begin to identify patterns and trends that will help you better understand what your customers are looking for.

An effective way to use analytics for product innovation is through customer feedback analysis. Customer reviews and feedback are an invaluable source of information about what works and what doesn't in your current products. By analyzing this feedback, you can identify areas for improvement and opportunities for innovation. For example, if multiple customers mention that they would like a specific feature in your product, this could be a sign that that feature is worth developing.

In addition to direct customer feedback, customer behavior analysis can also offer valuable insights. By studying how customers interact with your products and services, you can identify usage patterns and preferences. For example, if you notice that many customers use certain features of your product more than others, you can focus on improving and expanding those features. You can also identify customer segments that use your product in unexpected ways, which could open up new opportunities for innovation.

Benchmarking, or comparing products with competitors, is another useful technique. By analyzing your competitors' products, you can identify features and benefits that might be missing in your own products. This doesn't mean you should copy your competitors, but you can draw inspiration from their successes and learn from their mistakes. Analytics allows you to conduct this analysis systematically and objectively, based on hard data rather than subjective impressions.

Predictive analytics is another powerful tool in the innovation process. Using machine learning techniques and predictive algorithms, you can anticipate future customer needs and preferences. This allows you to develop products that not only meet current demands but also stay ahead of market trends. For example, if data indicates that customers are increasingly interested in sustainability, you can innovate by creating eco-friendly products that respond to this emerging demand.

Customer segmentation also plays an important role in product innovation. By dividing your customers into segments based on demographic characteristics, purchasing behaviors, and preferences, you can develop products specific to each segment. This allows you to customize your offering and better meet the particular needs of different customer groups. Analytics facilitates this process by providing detailed data on each segment and helping to identify niche opportunities.

Experimentation and A/B testing are effective methods for validating product ideas before launching them into the market. By prototyping and testing different versions of a product with groups of customers, you can gain data on which versions work best and why. This allows you to refine and improve your product before investing in full-scale production. Analytics helps you design and analyze these experiments, ensuring that decisions are based on solid data.

Innovation doesn't stop once a product is on the market. Continuous analysis of product performance and gathering customer feedback are crucial to keep improving and adapting your products. Analytics allows you to monitor the success of your products in real time and make quick adjustments based on current data. This gives you the flexibility to respond to changes in customer preferences and keep your products relevant in a competitive market.

Finally, analytics can also help you identify opportunities for co-creation with customers. By involving customers in the product development process, you can gain insights and perspectives you might not have considered. Not only does this improve the quality of your products, but it also strengthens your relationship with your customers by making them feel valued and heard. Open innovation platforms and online communities are great tools to facilitate this type of collaboration.

In short, using analytics for product innovation transforms the development process from something based on intuition to something guided by hard data. From collecting customer feedback to predictive analysis and experimentation, analytics provides the tools needed to create products that truly resonate with your customers. While the process may seem complex, the benefits of making informed, data-driven decisions are immense, and will allow you to maintain a competitive advantage in an ever-evolving market.

Return on Investment (ROI) Analysis

Understanding and analyzing Return on Investment, commonly known as ROI, is crucial to any marketing strategy. ROI measures the profit or loss generated by an investment in relation to its cost. Basically, it is a way of knowing if the money you are investing in your marketing activities is generating the desired results. Knowing ROI allows you to make informed decisions and adjust your strategies to maximize profits.

To calculate ROI, you need two key pieces of information: the cost of the investment and the revenue generated by that investment. The basic ROI formula is pretty simple: you subtract the investment costs from the revenue generated, then divide the result by the investment costs. Finally, you multiply by one hundred to get a percentage. For example, if you invest a thousand dollars in a marketing campaign and it generates two thousand dollars in revenue, your ROI would be (2000 - 1000) / 1000 * 100, which equals one hundred percent. This means you have doubled your initial investment.

Calculating ROI is just the first step. To truly understand the impact of your marketing investments, you need to dig deeper into the analysis. This is where ROI analysis comes in, helping you identify which campaigns and tactics are working best and why. This allows you to optimize your marketing budget and focus your resources on the most effective activities.

ROI analysis can be applied to different aspects of your marketing strategies. For example, you can analyze the ROI of your advertising campaigns on different platforms, such as Google Ads, Facebook Ads, or email campaigns. By comparing the ROIs of these different platforms, you can determine which one is most effective for your business and adjust your budget accordingly. If you find that your Google Ads ads generate a fifty percent ROI while your Facebook ads generate a twenty percent ROI, you might consider investing more in Google Ads to maximize your returns.

In addition to platform-based analysis, you can also perform ROI analysis by campaign type. This involves comparing the performance of different types of campaigns, such as lead generation campaigns, branding campaigns, or direct sales campaigns. Each campaign type has different goals and can generate different levels of ROI. By analyzing this data, you can identify which types of campaigns are most profitable for your business and adjust your strategies accordingly.

Another important aspect of ROI analysis is to consider time. Not all marketing investments yield immediate results. Some campaigns, especially those geared toward branding or building long-term relationships with customers, may take longer to show results. Therefore, it is important to continuously track and evaluate ROI over time. This will allow you to see the full picture and avoid hasty decisions based on short-term results.

In addition to financial ROI, you can also consider other types of ROI, such as ROI in terms of time or effort. For example, if a social media marketing campaign takes a lot of time and effort to run, but generates a low financial return, you might consider whether that time and effort could be used more effectively on other activities. By evaluating these different types of ROI, you can gain a more complete view of the value of your marketing investments.

ROI analysis can also help you identify opportunities for improvement. By breaking down the components of your marketing campaigns and analyzing what's working and what's not, you can find areas where you can optimize your strategies. For example, if you find that your Google Ads ads are generating a lot of clicks but few conversions, you could investigate why this is happening and make adjustments to improve the conversion rate. This could involve changing your ad copy, adjusting your audience targeting, or improving your landing page.

To perform effective ROI analysis, you need accurate tools and data. Marketing analytics platforms, such as Google Analytics, can provide detailed data on the performance of your campaigns. These tools allow you to track key metrics, such as cost per click, cost per acquisition, and conversion rates. By using these tools, you can gain clear insight into how your marketing investments are yielding results and where you can improve.

It's important to remember that ROI analysis is not a one-time event, but rather an ongoing process. The market and consumer behavior are constantly changing, so it's crucial to regularly review and adjust your marketing strategies. By continuously tracking ROI and making adjustments based on data, you can ensure that your marketing investments remain effective and profitable.

In addition to analytics tools, it's also helpful to set clear, measurable goals for your marketing campaigns. These goals give you a benchmark to evaluate the success of your investments and make adjustments based on the results. For example, if your goal is to increase sales by twenty percent in six months, you can use ROI to measure progress toward that goal and adjust your strategies if necessary.

In conclusion, ROI analysis is an essential part of any marketing strategy. It gives you a clear understanding of how your investments are generating results and helps you make informed decisions to optimize your marketing budget. By using analytics tools, continuously tracking, and adjusting your strategies based on the data, you can maximize your returns and ensure the long-term success of your marketing efforts.

Privacy in Marketing Analytics

In today's world, where marketing analytics plays a crucial role in business decision-making, data privacy has become a topic of utmost importance. Consumers are increasingly aware of how their personal data is collected, used and stored, and they expect companies to handle this information with the utmost care and transparency. Therefore, understanding and respecting privacy in marketing analytics is not only a legal obligation, but also a way to build trust and loyalty with your customers.

To start, it's essential to be aware of and comply with the data privacy laws and regulations that apply in your country or region. In many parts of the world, there are strict laws protecting consumer privacy, such as the General Data Protection Regulation in the European Union, known as GDPR, and the California Consumer Privacy Act, known as CCPA, in the United States. These laws dictate how personal data must be collected, handled, and protected, and the penalties for non-compliance can be severe.

The first step to ensuring privacy in marketing analytics is to obtain explicit consent from users before collecting their data. This means that consumers must be fully informed about what data is going to be collected, how it is going to be used, and with whom it is going to be shared. They must also be given the option to accept or reject this data collection. Using clear and simple forms to obtain this consent can help ensure that users understand and are comfortable with the process.

Once you have obtained consent, it is important to collect only the data that you really need. Not only can excessive data collection be seen as an invasion of privacy, but it also increases the risk of data breaches. For example, if your goal is to improve a specific marketing campaign, you do not need to collect irrelevant data such as users' personal address or contact information. Stick to collecting information that is directly relevant to your marketing goals.

Another crucial aspect of privacy in marketing analytics is the protection of the data collected. This involves implementing appropriate security measures to prevent unauthorized access, loss, or leakage of data. Some of these measures may include data encryption, use of strong passwords, implementation of firewalls, and regular employee training on data security practices. By taking these precautions, you can significantly reduce the risk of data breaches and protect your customers' sensitive information.

In addition to protecting data, it is also critical to be transparent about how it is used. Consumers have a right to know how their data is being used and for what purposes. Providing clear and accessible privacy policies on your website and at other customer touchpoints can help maintain this transparency. These policies should explain in detail how data is collected, used, stored and protected, as well as consumers' rights in relation to their personal data.

Data anonymization is another important practice to protect user privacy. This involves removing or altering personally identifiable information from collected data so that it cannot be associated with specific individuals. Anonymization allows companies to use valuable data for analysis without compromising user privacy. For example, instead of storing names and email addresses, you can use unique identifiers that do not reveal users' identities.

The right to be forgotten is another key aspect of privacy in marketing analytics. Under regulations such as the GDPR, consumers have the right to request that their personal data be deleted from company systems. It is crucial to have procedures in place to respond to these requests in a timely and comprehensive manner. By respecting this right, you are not only complying with privacy laws, but you are also demonstrating to your customers that you value and respect their privacy.

It's also important to educate your team on the importance of data privacy. All employees who handle personal data should be well-informed about the company's privacy policies and procedures. Regular training can help ensure that everyone understands their responsibilities and acts in accordance with privacy best practices. A well-informed team is a crucial line of defense against data breaches and other privacy-related issues.

Vendor and third-party management is another critical aspect of privacy in marketing analytics. If you work with third-party vendors who handle personal data on your behalf, it's essential to ensure they also comply with privacy laws and your company's policies. This may include conducting regular audits, signing data processing agreements, and continuously monitoring vendors' privacy practices.

Finally, maintaining a proactive attitude toward privacy can help you adapt to changing laws and consumer expectations. Data privacy is an ever-evolving field, and businesses must be prepared to adapt to new challenges and opportunities. By staying informed about the latest trends and developments in privacy, you can ensure that your company is always one step ahead and prepared to meet the highest standards of data protection.

In conclusion, privacy in marketing analytics is not only a legal obligation, but an opportunity to build trusting relationships with your customers. By obtaining proper consent, collecting only the necessary data, protecting information, being transparent about its use, anonymizing data, respecting the right to be forgotten, educating your team, properly managing vendors, and staying proactive, you can ensure that your marketing analytics practices are ethical, legal, and effective. This will not only protect your customers, but will also strengthen your company's reputation in the market.

Future of Analytics

The future of marketing analytics is full of promise and challenges. With technology evolving rapidly, companies have more tools than ever to understand their customers, optimize their marketing strategies, and make informed decisions. However, they also face complex questions about privacy, ethics, and the integration of new technologies. In this chapter, we'll explore how the future of marketing analytics is shaping up and what companies can do to prepare for these changes.

One of the most important trends in the future of marketing analytics is the increasing use of artificial intelligence and machine learning. These technologies make it possible to analyze large volumes of data faster and more accurately than ever before. Machine learning algorithms can identify patterns and trends that would be impossible to detect manually, allowing companies to personalize their marketing campaigns at a very granular level. For example, a company could use machine learning to predict which products certain customer segments are most likely to purchase and tailor their offerings accordingly.

Artificial intelligence is also improving marketing automation. Automated marketing platforms can use analytics data to send personalized messages to customers at the right time. Not only does this improve the customer experience, but it also increases the efficiency of marketing campaigns. Imagine a system that automatically sends emails with special offers to customers who have shown interest in specific products or retargets ads to users who have abandoned their shopping cart. These capabilities are becoming more common thanks to advances in artificial intelligence and analytics.

Predictive analytics is another area that is gaining traction in the world of marketing analytics. Through predictive analytics, businesses can anticipate future customer behavior based on historical data. This can include predicting future sales, identifying potential customer churn, or estimating demand for new products. Predictive analytics allows businesses to be proactive rather than reactive, giving them a significant competitive advantage.

Augmented reality and virtual reality are also beginning to have an impact on marketing analytics. These technologies offer new ways to interact with customers and collect data about their preferences and behaviors. For example, a furniture company could use augmented reality to allow customers to visualize what furniture would look like in their homes before purchasing it. At the same time, it could collect data on which products are most popular with different demographics and adjust its marketing strategies accordingly.

Another important trend is the growing importance of real-time data. In the past, many marketing decisions were based on historical data that could be outdated. Today, businesses have access to constant streams of real-time data, allowing them to adjust their marketing strategies instantly. For example, an e-commerce company can adjust its ads and promotions based on real-time purchasing behavior during special events like Black Friday. This ability to react quickly to market trends is a crucial competitive advantage in today's business environment.

Marketing analytics is also becoming more integrated with other areas of the business. In the future, we will see greater convergence between marketing analytics and sales analytics, financial analytics, and supply chain management. This integration enables a holistic view of the business and more informed decision making. For example, by combining marketing and sales data, a company can identify which campaigns are generating the most valuable conversions and adjust its budget accordingly.

Privacy and ethics will continue to be a crucial issue in the future of marketing analytics. With growing concerns about data privacy, companies will need to be transparent about how they collect, use, and protect customer data. They will also need to ensure that their analytics practices are ethical and do not invade user privacy. This may include using anonymization techniques to protect customer identity and compliance with data privacy laws.

The Internet of Things is another emerging technology that will have a significant impact on marketing analytics. With the proliferation of connected devices, companies will have access to an unprecedented amount of data about customer behavior and preferences. For example, a smart appliance company could collect data about how customers use its products and use this information to develop new features or improve the user experience. The ability to analyze data from a variety of sources in real time will be a key competitive advantage in the future.

Extreme personalization is a trend that will continue to grow. Consumers expect personalized and relevant experiences, and marketing analytics enables companies to meet these expectations. In the future, we will see an increase in the use of personalization to offer product recommendations, content, and offers specific to each customer. This not only improves the customer experience, but also increases the likelihood of conversion and loyalty.

Finally, marketing analytics will become increasingly accessible to businesses of all sizes. Data analysis tools are becoming more affordable and easier to use, allowing small and medium-sized businesses to reap the benefits of advanced analytics. This democratises access to information and levels the playing field, allowing more companies to compete effectively in the global marketplace.

In short, the future of marketing analytics is full of exciting opportunities. Artificial intelligence, machine learning, augmented reality, real-time data, and the Internet of Things are transforming the way businesses understand and connect with their customers. However, with these opportunities come challenges in terms of privacy, ethics, and data management. By keeping up with technology trends, being transparent and ethical in handling data, and using advanced analytics tools, businesses can fully leverage the potential of marketing analytics and ensure a successful future.

www.ingramcontent.com/pod-product-compliance
Lightning Source LLC
LaVergne TN
LVHW090416210926
848480LV00002B/591
9798230325949